Larger Than Life on Rollerskates:

A small selection of completely mad poems

By

Carolyn Davison

Copyright © Carolyn Davison 2009

The right of Carolyn Davison to be identified as the author of this work has been asserted by her in accordance with the Copyright, Designs and Patents Act, 1988

All rights reserved. This book is sold subject to the condition that it shall not, by way of trade or otherwise, be lent, re-sold, hired out or otherwise circulated in any form of binding or cover other than that in which it is published. No part of this book may be reproduced, whether by photocopy or by other means nor must any of the content be displayed on a website without prior permission from the author.

ISBN: 978-0-9561573-0-0

Contents

Larger than life on rollerskates

Hormones and aging

Yo ho ho and a bottle of something alcoholic and miscellaneous

Crazy Limericks

To my eldest son Tim, who spent many an hour with me laughing at my poems and helping me with the limericks and batty books.

To my youngest son Matthew, who spent many hours having to listen to Tim and I making up the limericks and batty books

To my dear husband, Alan, who has put up with me having my head in the clouds making up silly rhymes and stories all these years.

You are all so precious and special to me.

Larger Than Life on Rollerskates

ODE TO DIETING

Once I went to a party
My plate ladened with food
Well I didn't really want
To appear awfully rude

So on went the sausage rolls
Those little vol au vents
And I've got to admit it
Anything I would want.

The pizzas looked just scrummy
And the sarnies were a treat
The quiche looked rather special
And so did the sweet

There were cheesecakes and gateaux
Things oozing with cream
Everything looked delicious
I felt like I could scream

Who cares? I spooned it in
To my over-sized bowl
Everything in large quantities
Some things were whole

Oh well there's always tomorrow
To start on my slimming quest
I promise that tomorrow
I will do my uttermost best

The only problem is, you see
Tomorrow never comes
So if I'm not careful
I'll still be eating buns

Just pretend that somebody
Is paying you loads of dosh
If you lose all your excess weight
And don't eat too much nosh

Always think about being svelt,
Tiny and size eight.
And you could always go and buy
A tincey, wincey plate

Do not despair dear dieter
We all have ups and downs
So if you have a slip up
Don't wear those awful frowns

Brush it off and start again
Turn over a new page
Don't be angry with yourself
Don't fly into a rage

ODE TO DIETERS

I've lost 3lbs this dieting week
Onward to the next
Oh no I've got PMS
This will be a test

I've got a choc bar in the fridge
It stares me in the eye
I must be strong and resist it
Oh no I could really cry

I have a craving for it
I really must resist
But if I look in the fridge
It just seems to insist

I know, I'll go and exercise
I won't be bothered then
I'll be busy doing box steps,
And sit-ups, numbering ten

At last my hubby's home from work
I wonder if he wants a treat
Bye bye little chocolate bar
I know you're very sweet

But I just cannot eat you
Or my diet will be shot
And then the healthy eating
Really will be forgot

So sorry little chocolate bar
Sitting on the shelf
I must be really good
And kind to myself

I Can See Clearly Now

I can see clearly now my chest is gone
I can see all obstacles in my way
Gone are the tractor tyres from 'round my waist
It's gonna be a great great dieting day

I think I can make it now the flab is gone
I can see all parts of me melt away
Here is the weight loss I've been praying for
It's gonna be a great great dieting day

Look all around my BMI is normal now
Look straight ahead, I can see what's in front

I can see clearly now, my stomach's gone
I can see all shoes that are on my feet
Gone are the size 20 clothes now
It's gonna be a great, great dieting week

WHERE HAVE ALL THE FAT CELLS GONE?

Where have all the fat cells gone?
Long time burnt off
Where have all the fat cells gone?
Long time ago
Where have all the fat cells gone?
They've been jogged off, ev'ry one
   Oh, I feel slimmer now
   Oh, I feel slimmer now

Where have all the calories gone?
Long time disappeared
Where have all the calories gone?
Long time ago.
Where have all the calories gone?
In the gym and on the bikes
   Oh, I feel slimmer now
   Oh, I feel slimmer now

Where have all the biscuits gone?
Long time thrown away
Where have all the biscuits gone
Long time ago
Where have all the biscuits gone?
In a land fill ev'ry one
Oh, I feel slimmer now
Oh, I feel slimmer now

WOKE UP THIS MORNING

Woke up this morning, not feeling fine
Because I'd drunk a case of wine
My head was woozy as you would think
Something tells me I shouldn't drink

Woke up this morning, feeling big
I really wish I was like a twig
My stomach looked like a huge, round moon
Something tells me I should diet soon

Woke up this morning, feeling odd
I shouldn't have eaten the chips and cod
If I get bigger my clothes will be tight
Something tells me I should start eating right

Woke up this morning, feeling large
Because I'd eaten a tub of marg
If this continues I'll not fit in my jeans
Something tells me I should start eating beans

Woke up this morning feeling weird
I ate a cake which was 3-tiered
If I eat more then I'll just be sick
Something tells me, I need to diet quick

Woke up this morning feeling strange
My eating habits really must change
If I eat more then I'm gonna explode
Something tells me I'm a heavy load

GOOD KING WENCESLAS BUYS PIZZA

Good King Wenceslas went out
Bought pizza for Stephen
He ordered a big, round one
Deep pan, crisp and even.
Melted was the cheese on it
Stringy mozzarella
Stephen ate the whole lot up
Now he's a happy fella

DON'T CRY FOR ME HEALTHY SALAD

It won't be easy, you'll think it strange
When I just explain how I feel
That I still need the cake, after all I have lost
I just need chocolate
All I can feel is that I am so blue
My hormones are giving me gip
I understand and hope you do too

I had to let it happen, I had to eat
Couldn't stay all my life without junk
Looking into the cupboards and into the fridge
I need ice cream
Running around trying all of the brands
But none impressed me at all
Not even the one with choc chips

Don't cry for me healthy salad
The truth is, I will go and diet
And through my bad days
I'll always find ways
To lose all the flab
And not look too bad

And as for fig rolls, and as for crisps
I never meant to buy them in
Though it seems to the world they were all I desired
I preferred pizza
The cheese that's on top made me feel just so good
And the base was just crispy to chew
I understand and hope you do too

Don't cry for me healthy salad
The truth is I will go and diet
And through my bad days
I'll always find ways
To lose all the flab
And not look too bad

Have I eaten too much?
There is nothing more I can think of to eat today
But all you have to do is look at me
To know that I need to lose weight too

Don't cry for me healthy salad…

Biscuits in the Cupboard

Midnight
What's that sound from the cupboard?
Is it the chocolate digestives
All feeling alone?
In the dim light
They look just scrummy and yummy to me
And my stomach begins to moan

Biscuits
All alone in the cupboard
They would love some company
In my rumbling tummy
They could join the crisps and nuts I ate earlier on
Couldn't help it – they were yummy

Every packet
Seems to me to cry out a warning
My stomach grumbles
Then it starts a rumble
But soon it will be morning

Daylight
Should I wait for the sunrise?
Should I really have breakfast?
OH! I musn't give in
If I eat them
I'll feel like I've just given up
I will throw them in the bin

ODE TO CHOCOLATE

When I'm queuing to pay for fuel
You look so small and yummy
But I know if I eat you up
I'll get bigger on my tummy

Oh little thing in shiny paper
You look so very bold
But as my mother used to say
All that glitters is not gold!

50p in My Purse

I have a 50p
Stashed right in my purse
Shall I buy a fudge cake
Or something even worse?

Oh that yummy gateau
Just stares me in the eye
I need something sticky
I cannot pass it by

Just wait a mo!
Don't go on!
That's a zillion calories
Waiting to go on your hips
And even on your knees

Now how about a pack of gum
That's still sticky, you know
It'll glue your teeth together
And dinner you will forego

I thought about my waistline
And how I'd like to be thin
So there's my little 50p
Rattling in a tin!

EXERCISE BLUES

I started out on rollerskates
But landed on my rear
Everyone was laughing
And shouting "Hear, Hear!"

I changed over to a bicycle
One with many gears
I fell off more than I was on
And ended up in tears

So then I tried some mountain climbing
The tallest I could find
But my rope kept getting twisted
Which was rather a bind

I thought I'd try some badminton
What was the harm in that?
But when I tried to swipe the shuttle
I lost my blinkin' bat

I think I'll stick with DVDs
It's safer than the rest
I can prance when I want
And start feeling full of zest!

WHAT DO YOU WANNA SHOW THOSE PIES TO ME FOR?

What do you wanna show those pies to me for?
You know I'm trying to lose weight
It makes me mad, it makes me sad
Sometimes when I weigh myself I feel so bad

Quit fooling around with me now
I really don't want some pastry
Well that's alright I'll have low fat tonight
And baby you'll find the calories are just right

So what d'ya wanna show those pies to me for?
You know I'm trying to lose weight...

ODE TO CRISPS

Twas the night before weigh-in
And sat on the shelf
Was a packet of crisps
All by itself.
The flavour was cheddar
And onion too
I felt like I wanted them
At quarter past two

I got out of bed
And crept down the stairs
Hoping, just hoping
The pack was still there.
I opened the door
And peeked inside
There on the shelf
They sat with such pride

The shiny black packet
With writing so bold
Was a brilliant sight
Wondrous to behold.
My hand snuck in silently
To reach for the pack
I really, just really
Wanted a snack.

With stealth and precision
I opened the bag
And took a deep sniff
Oh what a drag!
I felt really guilty
My conscience kicked in
Should I decide to throw
Them all in the bin?

Oh what a dilemma
What should I do?
I fancied a snack
At quarter past two
I think I should trust
My instinct again
And throw them away
And never complain

So I opened the lid
And threw them right in
To join the biscuits
At the bottom of the bin!
Then upstairs I went
Feeling so smug
I got under the duvet
And felt really snug

Hormones And Aging

Planet Bodies

Why is it when we start to age
Gravity gets stronger
Our chests aren't pert anymore
And our legs get short, not longer?

Our rears hang down to the floor
And bounce when we skip
And when we bend to touch our toes
The sun begins an eclipse

Our stomachs are like a mini planet
Soon they will have a moon
It may have 2 or 3 or 4
If we don't start to diet soon

The rings around our middle
Would make Saturn very jealous
So let's all start to diet
Let's all be very zealous.

PMS Blues

My stomach has started bloating
I don't know what to do
Do I run around screaming?
Creating a hulla baloo?

Or do I sit down quietly
And listen to sweet sounds?
I hope at my next weigh-in
I haven't gained some pounds

Oh no I feel crotchety
I need some chocolate NOW!
And if I don't get any
I'll be a grumpy cow

So watch out all you husbands,
Partners, boyfriends too
If you saying anything rotten
We'll have to scream at you

Aren't hormones wonderful?
You can do as you please!
For one week in the month
Your guys beg on their knees

"Oh yes, my darling, you look great
When you wear that strapless dress!"
Your guy will say just anything
When under sweet duress

So come on girls, be strong and brave
And don't you ever cower
PMS is something which
Will give a girl her power

HORMONES

Hormones are wonderful, hormones are swell
Cause they can make ya happy and miserable as well
An' when ya on ya period, your men can always tell
When ya hormones are whizzing round ya body

REFRAIN
If it wasna for our hormones where would we be?
We'd be blobs of jelly, with no personality
Cause we wouldn't have the moods that swing, nor be grumpy
If we did na have the hormones in our bodies

And when we're on our monthlies, we wanna scream and shout
We lock ourselves in our rooms and keep our partners out
And when they yell – "You all right, love?" we wanna give em a clout
And then they all see we have some hormones

If it wasna for our hormones where would we be?
We'd be blobs of jelly, with no personality
Cause we wouldn't have the moods that swing, nor be grumpy
If we did na have the hormones in our bodies

Now when we get pregnant, our hormones go just wild
We want to eat everything, for the good of the child!
After birth with sleepless nights, it's easy to get riled
Because of the extra hormones in our bodies

If it wasna for our hormones where would we be?
We'd be blobs of jelly, with no personality
Cause we wouldn't have the moods that swing, nor be grumpy
If we did na have the hormones in our bodies

When we're young we have monthlies, then there's the menopause
Hot flushes and weight gain; water retention, of course
Then when we're low, we want to eat, perhaps a cow or horse
That's what we get for having flippin' hormones

If it wasna for our hormones where would we be?
We'd be blobs of jelly, with no personality
Cause we wouldn't have the moods that swing, nor be grumpy
If we did na have the hormones in our bodies

Yo Ho Ho
and
a Bottle of
Something alcoholic
and
Miscellaneous

Yo ho swabbys
Raise the Roger high
Come let's sail the ocean
Where the land meets the sky

Let's find buried treasure
On an island small or big
Let's go catchin other ships
And throw the crew in the brig

Yo ho Yo ho
A bottle of rum for me
Some mealie biscuits in a barrel
And some hard beef for me tea

Come on then me hearties
Dust down that musket of old
And let's go sailing round the world
For that cursed Aztec gold

Let's hear it for the parrot
Everyone say their oooo arrrrrs
And let's get them sails up
Come on you jolly tars

There once was a pirate called Ric
Whenever he sailed he was sick
Most of the ride
His head was over the side
And he didn't feel very slick

~~~~~~~~~~~~~~~~~~~~~~~

While sailing the ocean so blue
A pirate cap'n had a cockatoo
It sat on his head
They were sure he were dead
Of something they called the bird flu

~~~~~~~~~~~~~~~~~~~~~~~

There once was a pirate called Jed
He was so fierce all his enemies fled
They'd see him and run
And he thought it great fun
To put a big hole in his head

~~~~~~~~~~~~~~~~~~~~~~~

You've heard of the pirate red beard
All his mates thought he were weird
He thought it a blast
To sleep on the mast
Until one day it got sheared

The flute examiner

He sat there in the corner
Glasses poised upon his nose
Looking over the top of them
With a very superior pose

I raised my flute up to my lips
And gave a mighty blow
But nothing came out of it
And I went a healthy glow

He raised an eyebrow very high
He looked rather not amused
I tried again to get a note
But I was much bemused

The silly thing just wouldn't make
A beautiful haunting sound
So I gave it an almighty blow
And my cloth fell to the ground

I looked back at the man sat there
Not a smile upon his face
I thought I'd better play my tune
Before I left that place

So off I went again to try
And play my pretty tunes
This time I blew, a note came out
Not a minute or so too soon

My tune went loud then went quiet
Largo then Allegro
I had to play some chromatic scales
And one or two arpeggios

Up and down my scales I raced
Like a mighty rushing wind
My minors didn't sound too good
He looked like I had sinned

All through the exam
He sat and wrote
Upon his clean white pad
I wondered if he ever thought
I was good
Or bad

Thank you sir, I said to him
About to leave the room
When over his glasses, he looked at me
And in a mighty voice did boom

"But wait you cannot leave me yet
For you still have not finished!"
He played some notes and
I had to choose dominant or diminished

Shaking like a leaf I stood
By the grand piano forte
I really felt like I wasn't good
But very very naughty

He played a piece and I had to choose
Whether it was fast or slow
Or if it went very loud
Or had a dimin-u-endo

I breathed a huge sigh of relief
When he told me it had ended
I dropped my flute upon his foot
It's not what I intended

I picked up my flute
And hurriedly
Put it in its case
I threw my music into my bag
And ran fast from that place

For quite a while I had to wait
Before my results arrived
I'm happy to say
I passed that day
I got one hundred and five!

GUIDE CAMP (OR HOW TO GET RID OF YOUR CAPTAIN)

Once I went to guide camp,
Oh, it was a shambles
I hit my finger with a mallet
And ripped my dress on brambles

We tried to put our tents up,
But broke all the pegs.
Then we threw away our mallets
They hit our Captain's legs

We put up the fire screen,
But, alas, it got burnt down
Captain wasn't happy
Her face was just a frown

At last! It was time for lunch
A wasp was pestering me
I swatted it with my dinner plate –
It landed in Captain's tea

After lunch, that afternoon
There was a welly throwing comp.
I threw the Captain's welly
And it landed in the swamp.

Captain tried to retrieve it
Out of the mud and muck
But she leaned too far over
And in it, she was stuck

We threw to her a big long rope
She tied it around her belly
We pulled and pulled
She came out
And so did her welly

Later on we built rope bridges
Mine was very long!
But when Captain tested it
She found it not too strong

By six o'clock our tents were up
The pegs arrived that day
We thought it strange, while pitching them
Captain stayed away

That night we had a campfire sing song,
The flames were growing higher
We really hadn't intended
To start a forest fire.

We called the local fire brigade
With hoses they did come,
But by the time that they arrived
The damage had been done

The fire had spread to the campsite
All the tents burned to the ground
We were so shocked and frightened
We didn't make a sound

We had to go back home that night
We had nowhere else to go
Our spirits had been dampened
We were feeling very low

It affected our poor Captain
More than we can say
'Cause when we went to Guides again
She had moved away

There is a tiny rumour
That she may be in your town
So if you join a unit
Never make your Captain frown

She's there because she wants to make
You happy and well adjusted
Just behave and be very keen
So that you can always be trusted

BROWNIE PACK HOLIDAY

When I was a Brownie
I went on holiday
I didn't listen to Tawny Owl
'Cause all I did was play

The weather was appalling
It rained most of the time
The yard was full of puddles
And the field, full of slime.

There were spiders in the toilets,
And bugs in the shed
We were very frightened
And refused to go to bed

So we tied up Tawny's pyjamas
And sewed up her sleeping bag
We strapped her to the table leg
With the local Girl Guide flag

That night we had a midnight feast
We ate crisps and sweeties too
What a mess we did make
The mice joined us too!

One quiet, fine afternoon
We had a barbecue tea
I snagged and tore my Brownie dress
And scraped my little knee

The Camp Advisor came to visit
And stayed to have some food
We thought that we would play a trick
Which I admit, was very rude

She had a brand new sporty car
The kind without a top!
We let down all her expensive tyres
And filled it up with slop

We let her join in all our games
The welly throwing was 'brill!'
Until she saw her precious car
Then she gave us a hefty bill

Tawny Owl was very angry
Her face was scarlet red
And even though it wasn't late
She sent us all to bed

On the morning after
We all said we were sorry
Which didn't last, 'cause later on
We hijacked a lorry

Our group leader was driving
And having one big ball
Until she did a sharp right turn
And hit a farmer's wall

He ran out of his farm house
He was red and hopping mad
Tawny Owl had gone past angry
And told us we were bad

She said that she had had enough
She was looking old and grey
She phoned each of our parents;
To end our holiday

All forlorn we packed our bags
Tawny danced around
We waited for our mums to come
And didn't make a sound

We really did feel sorry
For all the things we'd done
But Tawny wasn't happy
So we missed out on the fun

When our mothers came to collect us
Tawny Owl's face had changed
She went from angry to happy
And didn't look deranged

Poor Tawny moved away from us
She went somewhere oversea
To live in a place that's nice and quiet
Far away from me

The moral of this story is
Plan your programme right
Or take along a defensive tool
And put up a worthy fight!

Limericks of all Sorts

Elizabeth I

There once was a queen called Liz
She never got in a tiz
She spoke French and Latin
Wore gowns made of satin
She really was the biz

Sir Francis Drake

There once was a sailor called Drake
Who was always on the make
He raided the king's beard
Which the Spanish found weird
But a joke, they could never take

Nero

There once was an emperor called Nero
He thought himself such a hero
He started the games
Put the loses heads in frames
Now everyone thinks he's a zero

Attila the Hun

There once was a Hun called Attila
Who liked munching on cavity filla
His teeth it did break
He couldn't eat steak
Now he's a cold-blooded killer

Vlad the Impaler

There once was a man called Vlad
Who was extremely bad
He liked playing with stakes
And wrestling with snakes
Now everyone thinks he's mad

Lady Godiva

There once was a Lady Godiva
Who bought all her clothes for a fiver
She decided to go nude
Which the people thought very rude
But boy, she was a good horse rider

King Edward I

There once was a king called Ed
Who wanted all the Scots dead
He killed a guy called Will
The Scots remember him still
They wish they could have his head

Elvis

There once was a singer named Elvis
Who liked to wiggle his pelvis
The youngsters would swoon
When he entered the room
Oh that great singer called Elvis

Pharaoh Seti

There once was a Pharaoh named Seti
Who rather liked eating spaghetti
He twisted it round
'Til his hands became bound
Then he fell off his royal jetty

Knight Gawain

There once was a knight called Gawain
Who everyone thought was insane
He rode into battle
Armed with a rattle
A pity he rode in, in vain

Trotsky

There once was a man called Trotsky
Who Stalin thought had a big plot-sky
He hunted him down
Iced-picked his crown
And now he is one big not-sky

Dick Turpin

There once was a guy called Dick Turpin
When he drank he would go a-slurpin
He held up a stage
And flew into a rage
Because it was full of green gherkins

RICHARD III

There once was Richard the 3rd
Who was a terrible nerd
He had a hunched back
So they called in the quack
Who prescribed him some lemon curd

BIGGLES

There once was a pilot called Biggles
Who flew his plane in squiggles
He shot down a Bosch
Made tons of dosh
And went to the bank full of giggles

DUKE OF YORK

There once was a Duke of York
Who was a tremendous dork
He ate curry for fun
Ended up on the run
But sorted it out with a cork

HORATIO NELSON

There once was man called Horatio
The French he loved to race-io
He raced them around all the Med
And shot them all dead
And never did lose any face-io

DUKE OF WELLINGTON

There once was a guy nicknamed Welly
He thought the French, very smelly
He campaigned in the west
And did his very best
And liked to eat lemon jelly

NAPOLEON BONAPARTE

There once was a guy Bonaparte
He liked to eat French tart
He stuffed it all in
Now he's not very thin
And boy, can that man fart!

WYATT EARP

There once was a man, Wyatt Earp
He went after an infamous perp.
He got in a fight
Came off not so light
And now he friends think he's a twerp

GENERAL CUSTER

There once was a General called Custer
Who sought all the Indians to fluster
He made a mistake
His scalp they did take
And made his superiors bluster

WILLIAM VI

There once was a king nicknamed Billy
His subjects thought him so silly
He rode around town
With his face in a frown
And shirt which looked rather frilly

King Philip of Spain

There once was a Spanish king, Phil
Who sought out Queen Liz, to kill
He raised an armada
He should have tried harder
And now the people think he's a pill

King Louis XVI

There once was a French king Louis
Who got into a right stewy
He lost his fine head
Cos the folks had no bread
And the royal line went down the loo-y

Peter the Great

There once was a Tsar called Big Pete
He had enormous feet
At over 6 foot
He wasn't a doot
But his brain just wasn't complete

IVAN THE TERRIBLE

There once was Ivan the Tsar
Who drove a very big car
He hit his son on the head
And he dropped down dead
He didn't get very far

ALEXANDER THE GREAT

There once was Alex the Great
His troops he would always berate
He sent them to war
He wanted lots more
In their eyes he no longer did rate

SCIPIO

There once was a general, Scipio
Who, confronted with elephants did flip-io
He beat Hannibal back
Gave him no slack
Neither did he take any lip-io

CALIGULA

There once was Caligula the nutter
Who was very partial to butter
Made his horse the pro-consul
So they took out his tonsil
And cast it away in the gutter

ELAGABALUS

There once was Elagabalus
Who wasn't very fabulous
He wanted to be
"A woman!" said he
And that got him into big troubulous

TIBERIUS

There once was an emperor, Tiberius
Who came across rather inferious
He lived on an isle
In spurious style
And became more and more nefarious

MARC ANTHONY

There once was a general called Tony
Who spoke a lot of baloney
He thought Cleo was great
Wanted her as a mate
But they both ended up on their own-y

MARCUS AURELIUS

There once was an emperor, Aurelius
In Germania he was rather serious
He fought all the tribes
Cos they didn't take bribes
But then he became quite delirious

PHAROAH KHUFU

There once was a Pharaoh called Khufu
Who very much liked eating tofu
Watched them build pyramids
With his myriad of kids
That dippy old Pharaoh Khufu

PAUL REVERE

There once was a guy, Paul Revere
Who yelled, "Hey the British are here!"
He rode his poor horse
'Til it tired out, of course
Then he stopped for a beer

GENERAL NEY

The once was a general called Ney
Who had a really terrible day
He charged all his men
Over again
But the guns kept getting in the way.

ADMIRAL VILLENEUVE

There once was admiral, Villeneuve
Whose ships kept having to swerve
Poor Nelson got shot
When the battle was hot
And the Brits said – "Oh what a nerve!"

ALAN

There once was a guy called Alan
Who drank more than a gallon
Of the finest dark ale
It made him turn pale
Oh that poor guy called Alan

TIM

There once was a lad called Tim
At maths no one beat him
He did fractions galore
Then called for some more
He definitely wasn't that dim

MATTHEW

There once was a lad called Matt
He didn't like wearing a hat
But he did wear a hood
Which made him feel good
What do you think of that?

DIZZY

There once was a woman called Dizzy
Who never seemed to be busy
She sat down all day
On the computer she'd play
And sometimes get herself in a tizzy

DOZY

There once was a cat called Dozy
Who was always very nosey
He squeezed into a drawer
We thought he was no more
But really he was kind of cozy

MINA

There once was Mina the cat
Who began to get very fat
She ate more and more
Couldn't squeeze through the door
Oh no! We can't leave her like that!

A bit about the author:

Carolyn was born in Cardiff and grew up in an area called Splott – yes it is a real area. She would spend many a day dreaming up poems and stories from quite a young age. The wackier the better!

Now married with two children and a cat she lives in West Wales, still dreaming up crazy stories and poems. She is a Christian and home educates her sons!

www.ingramcontent.com/pod-product-compliance
Ingram Content Group UK Ltd.
Pitfield, Milton Keynes, MK11 3LW, UK
UKHW041228200426
11947UKWH00034B/426

9 780956 157300